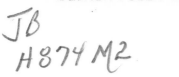

Langston Hughes

Great American Poet

Patricia and Fredrick McKissack

Series Consultant: Dr. Russell L. Adams, Chairman,
Department of Afro-American Studies, Howard University

Illustrated by Michael David Biegel

❖ *Great African Americans Series* ❖

Enslow Publishers, Inc.

40 Industrial Road	PO Box 38
Box 398	Aldershot
Berkeley Heights, NJ 07922	Hants GU12 6BP
USA	UK

http://www.enslow.com

To Carol Greene

Library of Congress Cataloging-in-Publication Data

McKissack, Pat, 1944–
    Langston Hughes : great American poet / Patricia and Fredrick McKissack.
       p. cm. — (Great African Americans series)
    Includes index.
    Summary: Simple text and illustrations describe the life of the Harlem poet whose work
gave voice to the joy and pain of the black experience in America.
    ISBN 0-89490-315-2
    1. Hughes, Langston, 1902–1967—Biography—Juvenile literature. 2. Afro-American po-
ets—20th century—Biography—Juvenile literature. [1. Hughes, Langston, 1902–1967. 2.
Poets, American. 3. Afro- Americans—Biography.]
    I. McKissack, Fredrick. II. Title. III. Series: McKissack, Pat, 1944– Great African
Americans series.
PS3515.U274Z677 1992
813'.5209—dc20
[B]   92-2583
                                      CIP
                                       AC

Printed in the United States of America

10 9 8 7 6

Photo Credits: The Archives Collection, Langston Hughes Memorial Library, Lincoln
University, Pennsylvania 19352, pp. 18, 26, 28; Library of Congress, pp. 4, 12, 21, 24.

Illustrations Credit: Michael David Biegel

Cover Illustration Credit: Ned O.

The following poems are reprinted by permission of the publisher, Alfred A. Knopf: "Color,"
From The Panther and the Lash by Langston Hughes, Copyright © 1967 by Arna Bontemps
and George Houston Bass; "Dreams," From *The Dream Keeper and Other Poems* by Lang-
ston Hughes, Copyright © 1932 by Alfred A. Knopf, Inc. and renewed 1960 by Langston
Hughes; and "My People," From *Selected Poems* by Langston Hughes, Copyright © 1926 by
Alfred A. Knopf., Inc. and renewed 1954 by Langston Hughes.

Contents

Langston Hughes
Born: Joplin, Missouri, February 1, 1902.
Died: New York City, May 22, 1967.

1

To Mexico and Back

It was very cold in Joplin, Missouri, the day Langston Hughes was born. And his father, James Hughes, was very angry. James had studied hard to become a lawyer in Oklahoma. But a new law said that African Americans could not be lawyers there.

James wanted to do better. He thought a black man could not live a good life in the United States. So he left his wife,

Carrie, and their baby, Langston, and moved to Mexico.

Carrie Hughes had been to college, too. Still, it was hard for her to find work. She and Langston had to move from place to place. At last she found a job in Kansas.

James opened a law office down in Mexico. He had lots of work. He was doing well. He asked his family to come live with him. Langston and his mother took a train to Mexico.

The day Langston and his mother arrived, there was an earthquake. The room shook. Mrs. Hughes screamed. She held little Langston closely. They had never been so frightened. Langston's mother said she would not stay another day in Mexico.

And she didn't. Langston and his

mother left on the next train back to Kansas. James would not come back to the United States. The Hughes never lived together again as a family.

2

Listening to Stories

Langston's mother worked at all kinds of jobs. Many times she didn't make enough money to buy food or pay the rent. So, when Langston was eight years old, he went to live with his grandmother, Mary Langston, in Lawrence, Kansas.

Langston missed his mother, but he loved his grandmother very much. She told wonderful stories about great African Americans like Frederick Douglass and Sojourner Truth.

The story he liked best was about Lewis Sheridan Leary. Lewis Leary was his grandmother's first husband. He was killed in 1859 at Harper's Ferry, Virginia. He had been part of John Brown's army. They had tried to help slaves fight for their own freedom. When Langston's grandmother told the story, she took out an old stained shawl full of holes. Lewis Leary had the same shawl with him when

he died. The story made Langston feel proud.

The Bible stories his grandmother told interested Langston, too. He also loved the hymns she sang.

There were not many black children in Kansas in the early 1900s. Langston was the only black child in his class. So he made friends with people in his books. He visited far-away and wonderful places by reading his books. He also wrote poetry and stories when he felt lonely.

When Langston was 12 years old, his grandmother died. For two years after that he lived with people he lovingly called Auntie and Uncle Reed.

Then Langston's mother married Homer Clarke. Langston went to live with them. He liked his stepfather very much.

It was good to be home with his mother again.

Langston finished grade school in Lincoln, Illinois. Then Homer got a job in Cleveland, Ohio. Going to school there was much more fun for Langston. Children in his class were from different races and from other countries, too.

Cleveland in 1916 was a fast-growing city. Langston graduated from Central High School there.

3

Deep Like the Rivers

When Langston was in high school he heard from his father, James Hughes. He wanted Langston to spend the summer with him in Mexico. Langston was surprised. He had not heard from his father in years. Langston went to Mexico on the train.

James had done very well. He owned a big ranch and had lots of workers. But James was a bitter and angry man. He said unkind things to people. When summer was over Langston was happy to go home.

Langston graduated from Cleveland Central High School in 1920. His father wanted him to come back to Mexico. Langston went because he needed help to go to college.

On his way to Mexico he crossed the Mississippi River. The dark water made him think about his race. So he wrote a poem called "The Negro Speaks of Rivers." It began: *My soul has grown deep like the rivers.*

The poem was printed in *The Crisis* magazine in 1921. For the first time, many people got to read his poetry.

James Hughes decided to pay for Langston's college. He sent him to study mining engineering at Columbia University in New York.

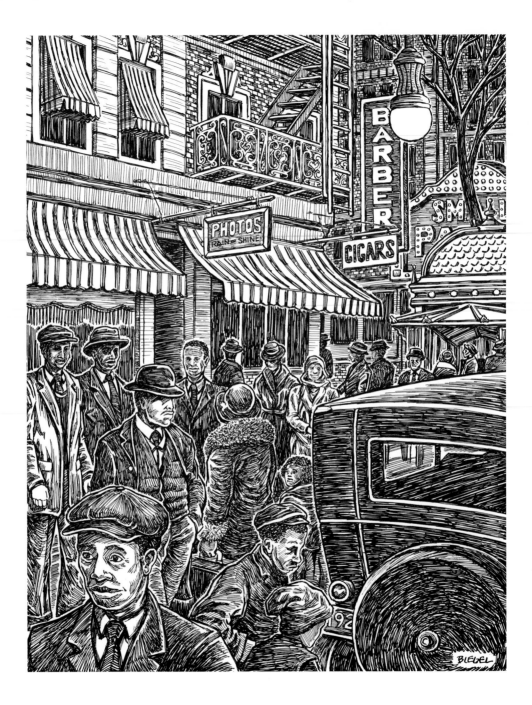

Near Columbia University is a mostly black neighborhood called Harlem. Living close to Harlem made Langston feel part of a large black family. He enjoyed being around African Americans. He liked the sounds and smells, the music and dance, the way people talked to each other. He decided to live in Harlem and write about it.

He wrote the poem "My People" to show how much he loved being black:

The night is beautiful,
So the faces of my people.

The stars are beautiful,
So the eyes of my people.

Beautiful, also, is the sun.
Beautiful, also, are the souls of my people.

During the 1920s thousands of African Americans moved to New York City, seeking a better life. Langston was part of that great migration.

4

The Weary Blues

Langston loved New York, but he didn't like school. He soon quit. Langston never heard from his father again. When James Hughes died, he didn't leave his son anything. Langston felt sorry for his father, because he had been such a sad and lonely man.

When Langston was twenty-one years old he joined the crew of the S.S. *West Hesseltine*. The ship sailed from New York to West Africa. Young Langston was excited about seeing the places he had read about in books.

Africa was exciting. So were many of the people he met. The bright clothes, music, and dancing of Africa made him think of Harlem. He wrote "Color," a poem that says African Americans should be proud of their skin color:

Wear it
Like a banner
For the proud
Not like a shroud.
Wear it
Like a song
Soaring high
Not moan or cry.

After he left Africa, Langston went to Holland, and then to Paris. He worked hard washing dishes and scrubbing floors. But he always found time to write.

Finally Langston's travels brought him back to New York. The first place he went

Langston loved art and music almost as much as he did writing.
In this picture he is holding a piece of Mexican art.

was to Harlem. He laughed for joy! He felt at home.

Langston's mother was living in Washington, D.C. at that time. He wanted to be near her, so he moved there in 1925.

Langston worked as a busboy at a hotel in Washington. Once, a very famous poet named Vachel Lindsay was staying at the hotel. So, Langston put some of his poems next to the poet's dinner plate.

Later that night, many people came to hear Vachel Lindsay read his poems. He read Langston's poems, too. He said he had discovered a new poet.

Newspapers across the country wrote about Lindsay's poetry reading. Soon many people knew about the new black poet, Langston Hughes.

Langston wrote mostly about Harlem and the interesting people who lived there. He wrote ten volumes of poetry, sixty short stories, two autobiographies, and several dramas during his life. He also wrote *Simply Heavenly*, a Broadway play about his favorite character, Jesse B. Semple.

5

Harlem's Poet

In 1926 Langston won a prize for his first book of poems, *The Weary Blues*. His poems were about Harlem life.

The Great Depression began in 1929. Times were very hard. Black people left the South and came North looking for work. But there were no jobs.

During the 1930s Harlem became overcrowded. People were hungry and angry. Many were homeless. Langston wrote about the people he saw on Harlem

Langston decided to go back to college in 1927. He graduated from Lincoln University in Pennsylvania in 1930. Lincoln is one of the oldest schools for African Americans in the United States. It was started in 1854.

streets, in churches, in schools, in clubs. He wrote about their pain and joy. He wrote about their anger and love.

Langston kept writing during the 1940s and 1950s. He always enjoyed the music of Harlem. He invited musicians to play jazz, spirituals, and blues music while he read his work in public. His poetry was like music.

During the 1950s, Langston wrote about Jesse B. Semple, who everybody called "Simple." Even though he was not a real person, he seemed real.

Simple had a way of saying funny things that sometimes had a serious meaning. People liked reading about this down-to-earth man who worked hard and lived in Harlem. Simple knew how to enjoy life, even if he didn't have a lot of money.

Langston had written over five Simple books by 1957. Langston also wrote two books about his own life: *The Big Sea* and *I Wonder As I Wander*. And he won many awards.

Langston traveled to many of the places he read about as a child. But most of all, he liked coming home to 127th Street in Harlem. He did such a good job of writing about the people who lived in this neighborhood that he was sometimes called "Harlem's Poet." But Langston Hughes belonged to all Americans.

Langston won many awards for his writing. In 1959 he won the Spingarn Medal given by the National Association for the Advancement of Colored People.

He wrote until he died on May 22, 1967. A jazz band played at his funeral. He had told his friends not to be sad. He wanted them to keep working for the better world he dreamed about. Today, Langston Hughes' poetry still sings to us about dreams:

Hold fast to dreams
For if dreams die
Life is a broken-winged bird
That cannot fly.

Hold fast to dreams
For when dreams go
Life is a barren field
Frozen with snow.

Words to Know

blues—Music about everyday joys and sorrows.

earthquake—A clashing of the Earth's deep underground plates, which cause the earth's surface to shift and move. Earthquakes destroy buildings and homes, and many people are often killed.

graduate—To complete a course of study at a school, and receive a degree.

Great Depression, The— Many people lost their jobs and homes beginning in 1929. It was hard for people to pay for food, homes, and other things they needed. Many people were poor and unhappy until the Depression ended with the start of World War II.

Harlem—A mostly black neighborhood in New York City. During the 1920s and 1930s many black poets, writers, and artists lived and worked there. This time was called the Harlem Renaissance.

jazz—Music used to show feelings and ideas and is mainly performed with instruments.

mining engineering—Mining engineers figure out the best way to get ore and oil out of the ground and out of rock so it can be used by people. Gold is an example of an ore.

poetry—A form of writing that uses any combination of colorful words, rhythm, and rhyme, written in verse. This kind of writing uses images or word pictures to express powerful emotions and ideas.

slaves—People who are owned by other people and are forced to work without pay. In America, slavery lasted from 1619 to 1865.

spirituals—Religious songs that were sung by black slaves. Now they are enjoyed and sung by people all over the world.

Index